The Net

Also by Daniel Tobin

Poetry

Where the World Is Made (1999)
Double Life (2004)
The Narrows (2005)
Second Things (2008)
Belated Heavens (2010)

Criticism

Passage to the Center: Imagination and the Sacred in the Poetry of Seamus Heaney (1999)
Awake in America (2011)

As Editor

Light in Hand: Selected Early Poems of Lola Ridge (2007)
Poet's Work, Poet's Play: Essays on the Practice and the Art (2007 with Pimone Triplett)
The Book of Irish American Poetry from the Eighteenth Century to the Present (2008)

The Net

Daniel Tobin

Four Way Books
Tribeca

Please direct all inquiries to:
Editorial Office
Four Way Books
POB 535, Village Station
New York, NY 10014
www.fourwaybooks.com

Library of Congress Cataloging-in-Publication Data

Tobin, Daniel.
[Poems. Selections]
The net : poems / by Daniel Tobin.
pages cm
ISBN 978-1-935536-40-6 (alk. paper)
I. Title.
PS3570.O289N48 2014
811'.6--dc23

2013036091

This book is manufactured in the United States of America and printed on acid-free paper.

Four Way Books is a not-for-profit literary press. We are grateful for the assistance
we receive from individual donors, public arts agencies, and private foundations.

NATIONAL
ENDOWMENT
FOR THE ARTS

This publication is made possible with public funds from the National Endowment for the Arts.

[clmp]

We are a proud member
of the Council of Literary Magazines and Presses.

Distributed by University Press of New England
One Court Street, Lebanon, NH 03766

CONTENTS

For of meridians, and parallels,
Man hath weaved out a net, and this net thrown
Upon the heavens, and now they are his own.

John Donne, "An Anatomy of the World"

THE JETTY

reaches, a stone sentence, across the bay—

its jigsaw syntax entered like hopscotch
from Lands End,
                    entered the way wrens
step, step on sidewalks, crushed shells,
looking for seed,
                    as if unsure of earth–

until it feels natural to be outside
the known scope,
                    and you follow
the jumbled puzzle out farther

than you first expected, toehold
by toehold,

                    to where the broader slabs
give certain footing, a way over water,

Appian, you think, miraculous
the way it seems to float
                            on tidal flats,
beach grass wavery as prairie
sprouting from wavelets, tinselate,

the whole horizon threatening to blend
earth, sky, and sea,
                    though sea, sky, and earth

stand poised, pristinely, on the glinting
edge,
        so you come to feel yourself
suspended in a fluency that would be

ethereal if not for the *thump, thump*
of a festival drumming intermittently

from the town, over parabolic sands,
like finest brushstrokes lacing the shoals—

shallows of moon snails, welks, skate eggs,
these currents like sandcoils redoubling

in pools where shucked pilings, scarified
granite,
        brace to colonies of rockweed
that flail in sediment's plangent ooze,

the soft siphons of lowlier lives
shooting invisibly from under,

trumpet worms, dogwinkles, bits
of swamp pink and poverty grass

awash in foam the color of meringue,
salt spray rust in the tide's
                        recursive flow,
a slow parting-of-the-waters revealing

articulations of tablets into shifting

4

dunes that have arranged themselves

into just this measure, as if to say
Nothing needs you here—
                              not the sundews
and sanderlings, plovers, hovering gulls;

not even the lighthouse at Long Point,
a beacon at the brink of the human:

you are an earthstar tumbling its spores
into the living waste,
                            the risen pleroma,

your name a net caught in the hollow
between stones
                        while the tide sounds
the length of this transit, susurrant

fountain, a summoning from under,
and all of it gone by evening.

A STONE IN ABERDARON

The poem in the rock and
the poem in the mind
are not one . . .

R. S. Thomas

Driving the Llyn, our tongues backed to teeth,
Speaking the palette / like Bushmen,
Soft click of a key sticking in language,
We navigate coastal roads in rain

Where the Atlantic shambles to Hells Mouth
And Whistling Sands—wind-stanched pilgrims
Sped out of the past by some fleet machine
To this shearwater church on the sound:

Your sound, your church—an eyrie at the crux
Of the human village and the sea,
Ancient fields weathered into bracken, brine,
The membrane of this shingle shore,

Runnels of foam in the slow tidal hush.
Obstinate priest, rock-faced, you listened
For the presence of your God like a pulse
Thrumming in the offing's ashen verge,

A whisper in the fleece of gunshot clouds.
Even now, chin deep in world, I love
Your raw vigil at the mirror's plunge,
Your rapt loneliness before the fathoms.

Here, under Hywyn's double nave, for years
You raised in faith the gleaming zero
Of the chalice rim. In the chancel's womb
You felt Christ like gritstone in the host.

For you the mind honed itself on this edge,
Your slate sublime hardened to a gem
Underground, resistant to thought, to song,
The threadbare scripts of keen equations,

Our vagrant shrines of the passing species,
And history pitiable as grass
Dunged by lost droves, while grace ran, a river
Disappearing down a swallow hole

To surface—your maker's rage, your longing—
In the depths: intimate immensity
That left you grim and brooding on the hills,
Your prayers signals beamed through shattered glass.

God was a raptor hunting you at night,
The brute vacuum portioned between stars,
Nameless well of sourceless light, sky's window,
And bone's rapture at the curtain's breath.

Your ashes scattered among these swells
Have mingled in the seething grottoes
Below bare cliffs, the seawall slicked green
As in some pre-Silurian dawn.

And there, in the scoured shallows, this stone
Big as a room, washed as if by microns
Ashore, bright-flecked, emerald, amazing.
We feel around it for the miracle

It is—rune of Earth, capsule of pure time,
Lobe of the Godhead's adamantine brain.
What would you have conjured from the gift
As day's first bathers dive into the surf?

THE STILL POINT AT CRAIGVILLE BEACH

High above the coast and flashing ocean
where the bathers gather to stipple their feet
    with licks of surf, or take the dive,
and two boys fling their Frisbee (its motion
    something between skeet
and a hovercraft's skittering glide)

someone—it's you—leans over the
wooden porch rail of a lodge like the bow
    of that tanker churning along
the edge where sky comes down to water.
    Someone right now
could be looking back from his own sin-

gular perch, eying on shore the outline
of a bluff where they picture someone
    else scanning the horizon.
And if each of them were able to mine
    something of the other one
in themselves, perhaps the next bright wind

would carry hints of these elsewheres across
the glittering distance—the vacationer,
    arms folded like a genii's
against his chest, and the one who passes,
    head cast like a coin on
the portal—you, you again, in reverie.

Meanwhile, presiding over its salt marsh,
fabulous as some outsized jungle bloom,
    the great blue heron turns
downward, inward, looking past its image
    in an undulant room.
Then wings lift. Rushes. Unremarked and gone.

OVID IN THE AGE OF TIN

Now that all the fluent bodies have morphed
into the their destinies' skins—bark or feathers,
or some lizard's earth-caressing scales—
and Tomis is a banished memory,
a bad vacation beside the Black Sea,
I can wander unacknowledged among
this modern breed with their appendages:
a window in the palm on which the sky
opens to the strains of an Orphic song
or, more often, something closer akin
to the yelps of dogs or maenads tearing flesh.
Others, chittering, perch in urgent hands,
and there are fingers I've seen that race
over black slate hieroglyphs, the raised pads
the trail they follow—Sisyphus on his hill,
or an eager, determined animal
tantalized by its own vigor on the wheel
that goes and goes and goes and goes nowhere.
I've watched them on the streets in their solitudes
as if each were the haunted flower of themselves
awash in the pool of their own regard,
the pods in their ears tailing to the box
that hangs from their necks, through which the god
speaks who makes them jitter with his might
and mouth his words. At night, they turn inside
where a greater portal opens onto realms
and they sit in conclave, deities at ease
whose judgments have no traffic with those shapes,
though they flicker brightly, one world to the next
at thumb press or nod—laughter, shouts,
the mounting gabble of jabbering heads.

And that parade of beasts with goggle eyes,
those rumbling Minotaurs, the shrieking eagles
reigning down flames like planets on anthills,
rigged compresses of dung that butcher the crowd,
none of it alters our kind by an atom.
Age of Iron, Age of Bronze, Age of Gold.
No one can reel back the regress of our march,
and the gods' flood comes to level all things new.
I would be grateful for another flood.

A STARRY MESSENGER

In the layers of one deep ravine scientists discovered evidence of "shocked quartz," indicative of an asteroid strike.

National Geographic, *Naked Science*

   This abyssal seam
Shocked white, all matter blanching
   As though at once the planet

   Glimpsed the shrieking face
And its ossifying coif
   Of serpents snapping

   Through the atmosphere—
Six-mile flint head, galactic
   Pinball, tumbling for eons

   Through the post–Big Bang gambit,
Gizmo singularity
   That (if you incline

   Anthropic) tips the
Euclidean dice toward us,
   Oh provident Yucatan,

   Knocking off the big critters,
Raising up the furry runts
   Sleight by mutant sleight

Until we arrive,
Eve's garrulous clan, fallen
    Tree-huggers, inveigling

The long grasses with our grunts,
Striding on upright haunches
    Into piazzas

Where torched bonfires burn
Their living human tinder—
    How quickly time's pass-

Age from opposable thumb
To disposable sums—while
    The watchman stares

Into tracks of stars,
Calculating amplitudes,
    Surveying the hushed sublime

As in a bright gallery,
Someone imagines being
    The hand on the brush,

The gaze of the world
The eye makes just by looking
    Remade in the practiced room—

So we know it is only
Our own strayed immensity
    Caught in the signals,

Our own rogue future
Hurtling almost toward us in
   The telescope's cosmic eye,

Lodestar whirled from the vacant,
Grazing air like a skipped stone
   In endless ocean,

Or a contraption
In Rube Goldberg's universe,
   The immense design of play

That, sometime, will wallop us
When how many billion lives
   Spin in their orbits

On a day like this,
Each one with everyone gone,
   Gathered inside the marrow—

Yes, it could be tomorrow
When the lodestone mote bears down
   And life wobbles on.

DOUBLE EXPOSURE

Belfast

As the Gods Who All Things Know

You would save the harrowed from their foregone fall,
as though a wish could mend a broken seal,

the numb wound sharpen its nerve again, to heal
clean back to its raw complaint. The angel

at the gate beyond the impasse wields his peace,
a flaming sword stanched tamely in its sheathe,

still flauntingly phallic, but secreted as the
dream of some hidden, heaven-presiding face.

You keep this filtered vigil and endure
the blindfold's vista, the TV's chattered light,

glimpse the fruit intact on its unbleeding tree.
Too much: a neat drink, and arm the door.

You, at least, are well who have beheld the sign
that hawks how each day's work will bring its ease.

With a Glint of the Red Horse

The wind in the flue like a great sheet luffing.
Or is it the flag of the *Geist*'s disposition,
its wing flap unbattened in the jet stream's trough?

Across slate rooflines clouds rove in Kevlar.
Armies watch them pass through goggles bright with jaundice.
When the seas incline to rise, will fish be their semaphore?

With *factional* rhyme *fictional*, with *sin, synopsis*.
With *trope* rhyme *entropy*, with *godhead* rhyme *goaded*.

Your hand in another's is all you know of Aves.
Home without a hearth leaves the universe stranded
where larvae consume a beech bole's thriving summa.
A flatworm in marl is the Earth's next genesis.

With *murmur* rhyme *memory*, with *shockwave* rhyme *salve*.
With *thresher* rhyme *threshold*, with *end* rhyme *and*. . . .

"AND NOW NOTHING WILL BE RESTRAINED FROM THEM"

Genesis 11:1–9

Life in our fortified huts brooks easy, though wind
bears down, bears up under heaven's *frumwoerc*
with its formidable *fyr* guttering earthward
from the sky-road again—a rocket's weird glare?
The pixel-hearth warms, coddled as we are,
while behind us our assay with its hoards
rudders on: the worm of us with our man-price,
word-price, and all the far *tofts* diminishing

whomever the *wealas*, whomever the "stranger."
And we, strangers to the strangers in ourselves
shadowing us through the thickets of language
like the code of some lost, primordial cousins
watching their *terminus* stride across the tundra,
fare forward with mongrel, omnivorous tongues,
adaptive, flagrant. *To enchain syllables, and to lash*
the wind are equally the undertakings of pride

Dr. Johnson wrote. Though to lash and enchain
or, as Webster mused on this late shore, to enjoin
some intercourse with tribes, in Europe wholly unknown
keeps the dulcet prow buoyant on its course.
Kayak, totem, chipmunk, moose, tote, banjo, juke,
make their music in the Native Grand Opera
with *schlep, hex, hoodlum, shanty. Brogue*-speakers sport
a shodden tongue, but it skips on, and *bling*

has become *de facto*. While far off, the Monchak
slog into wastes, *chochtar*, against the current,
their one of many words for *go* before they're gone.
And the Nivk with their multiple names for pairs
decouple from the planet's itinerant train.
Come back, Pomo, with your computation by sticks,
infinite sticks in the mind, your great woven creel,
the last ten of you subtracting, *k'ali*, to none.

In Siberia the Tofa, just thirty of thousands left,
still round their lives by the moon's nomadic light,
Hunting with Dogs Month, Gathering Birch Bark Month,
and ride the castrated reindeer beyond the ice to join
the Morovo, where the snake they call *ground-fish*
parses to a school that aggregates, *uduma*, to a
single body, or moves, *sakoto*, the way mourners
in procession almost undulate in their grief.

Always these grim goings—how the women
keen over their bombed, their broken, *Habibi*,
and the world become suddenly unspeakable.
You can see it, now, in the shelled look of the girl
cradling her fiancé back from war, his skull
a fissure where the shrapnel shrieked its expletive;
can *hear* it in those primal stares without sound,
huddled forms in a cave by the edge of a wood—

Habibi, Oh my Beloved, Oh my Dear One.

PARASITICAL

Despite having no lungs of its own body, the second head displays signs of independent consciousness.

                              The first fiction is
                          I'm talking to you at all,
                              the more amorphous
                      of my own Janus head, the god
                          alive and compassing
                      what has gone and what
                              is coming, though
                          which is which is
                          hard to say. Did I say
                      my own? I meant ours, my
                          sister twin, the comelier
                  countenance of our mirror
                      linkage, orbital, locked,
                          each turned away one
                      from the other, turned
                          outward each to our
                          own horizon, inverted
                  reflections on the knife-
                  edge of a pane. Don't be
                      distracted by my lack
                          of a body, the froth
                      at my mouth, my eyes
                      circling in their sockets
                  like wobbling stars, I, too,
                  keep counsel in our shared
                  skull, the woven vessels
                  of our thoughts, the mutual

current of our separateness.
Her limbs, her length, are mine,
wayward from me outwardly,
and if you call me the one
who follows, dependent,
the monster in the blood,
think of your own, the seamless
bonds inside your boundaries
hidden familiarly; think
how each breath lives
off another's, so that in
another world, another time
we two together, one, would be
divinity in human form,
holiest, a double sun, the crown
of the temple's plenum, and I
something more than a mask
you cut free for love
of the other, who of course
will die without me; the visage
in the bottom of the tray
you'll bury to salve yourselves—
the scar, the scald, the waste,
the link, the lack: your secret face.

FLY AND CRICKET

Its ear attunes homage to those wings
that would entice a consort's tailored song.

Where carapace affects a telephone
it listens beyond longing's least unease

to hear inside a trigger-scale of notes
like a rapper's staccato hail of words—

the key that calls the quiet gamut out
writhing, to burrow in the singer's gut.

Down there what governs and endures is this:
a screeching in the music of the spheres

where one of all that symphony will feed
on living meat until the husk exhumes.

So out pulses shroud-faced Eurydice
with Orpheus's body for its womb.

THE BEARDED LADY AT THE SQUEALING PIG

Thirsty Thursdays—all of the fluent bodies
morphing to the skin of a single creature,
though my friend here saw you coming through the crowd.
You've seen her at the Center? She said you might.
You have that look of someone looking
ahead of himself for a face you can't quite place,
but which you know is known to you. Not me,
I'm sure. I can tell that I'm not your type.
You're not the kind to go for a woman
with a buzz cut and plush Homeric chin.
Like how my cowgirl blouse shows off my tits?
Ovid knew best. *Hirsute* sounds like *her suit*,
and there's no one better than Tiresias for swinging
both ways.
                    Yes, that's right, like she said, this town
can absorb anything. When I first came
it was as though I had found my latitude
on an island of wide enchantments,
so no need for imperiled journeys home.
I preferred the libidinous alterations,
the dance floor's fisted beat, the leather alleys.
You've seen how these streets nestle down into bay,
recline into dunes, ocean surrounding,
the sands sifting through beach grass—what's the word?
Protean, right, everything protean,
and the sky changing, too, without judgment.
Can I buy you one?
                    You should hit the galleries,
Heller's, my favorite—Averys, Motherwells.
I love the rawness, the monumental nudes.
Better, come to my parlor. I had a swan

walk in the other day. Gloves. A veil.
She didn't strip. She disrobed. Her skin
was a lavish canvas she paid me to unfold
with needle and ink, a floating world,
a lucent mural tumbling down her flanks.
For myself I like to keep it simple—
this barbed wire around my forearm, a crown
of thorns. Have you ever thought about tattoos?
Yes, men do when they're drunk. A cross? A rose
would suit you better
                                        right here, above the wrist
where the hairs grow softest. I do piercings, too.
Why wait for a god's lust to goad the trans-
figuration? Tongue rings and nipple studs,
the crimson thrall of scarified faces,
these invoke what those airy ghosts would know:
themselves in us. And the Burmese women,
the Kayan, have you seen the photographs,
their necks coiled in brass year after year
till they stretch impossibly from their bodies?
It's the dragon mother coming to life
in their lives, with their bodies, through their bones.
Fashionable? It's the way gods fashion us
as we fancy that we fashion ourselves.
Burma lifts in brass, we preen in silicon,
but when the surgeon left and what was me
was gone, I felt my new crotch glowing
from the inside like an orchid by O'Keeffe.

Would you like another? I do hope so.
Has anyone said you have Etruscan lips?
It's all transformation. Above my bed
I've pinned a poster of Saint Sebastian,
the Guido Reni, his phallic arrows
quivering as he gazes in ecstasy,
the spirit's release a louche martyrdom.
And always I've marveled how the Doubting
fingers the vaginal wound of the Risen
to be sure of what aches beyond the known.

You have to teach tomorrow? Just one more.
My friend would like to know you better.
The night is young and you're so beautiful,
I'd hear my father say to my mother
before sleep, without a note of sarcasm.
Tell us about your poems, what obsesses you.
You came in for a drink, now you're the rage.
Don't let your head float away from us downstream.
We'll sit, attentive stones, on these two stools,
our blood like mounting drums with every word.

THE EDGE

Those nights my mother drank until she'd drop,
she'd rail against her husband, her sons, her life—
No bones left over in a butcher shop.

It was her gall, her private agitprop,
the protest pill against her bristling grief.
On nights my mother drank until she'd drop,

the kitchen bulb burned glumly like a prop
in her personal Beckett play—comical strife?
No. Bones. Left over in the butcher shop

of her malaise, I'd swab a sullen mop
across the floor of myself and gnaw the tripe
those nights my mother drank, until she'd drop

years later into the sleep that doesn't stop;
or if it does, it does where balm is rife,
no bones left. Once, inside a butcher shop,

I watched the clerk behind the counter strop
marrow into diamonds with a carving knife.
Most nights my mother drank until she'd drop.
No bones left over in a butcher shop.

THE MIDGES OF LETTERFRACK

St. Joseph's Cemetery, Industrial School

We walk up the hammered concrete flight
to the gate with its rope latch and black cross
and stand, quiet, before the graves of the lost
boys, beaten, who died here, kept out of sight
for years in these beds, for years unnamed.
In new shops apprentices are turning wood,
in yards the poppies burst like risen blood,
and above us summer's rare azure deepens.

Here, the smoky glint of each plaque burnishes
its charge to the sun, and suddenly they come
dartingly at us, a surge whispering,
infinitesimal, from some hidden scrum,
their wounds in us needling before they fade,
their hum in our ears. And nothing to say.

MECHANISM

The icemaker doesn't make ice.
Each day, at precise intervals,
the couple can hear the mechanism

move through its cycles—sudden buzz
as though inside a hand turned a switch
that freed the current from its bolt,

its hum sliding past grommet and sleeve;
then the sensor arm snapping down,
announcing the cold arrival.

Like the freezer had laid an egg.
And no climate to fix the machine
that fills and fills its empty tray
for years in the childless kitchen.

SMALL ODE ON A WAVE FUNCTION

*The mind reels when one realizes that . . . all possible worlds
co-exist with us. . . . This means that the waves of each world
vibrate at different frequencies and cannot interact anymore.*

Michio Kaku

On the bright other side of the wormhole
where the lives we might have lived live on,
swirling droplets in night's entire sea,
    you're like a sea creature that walked the Earth,
       unaccustomed stranger, until it chose
        a future of fins, a memory of song.

     How else should I summon you into my song
    who never was, who never will be whole
or partial to the world, this world we chose?
The fin, the finger, and the face live on
   in body's codes, amenable as Earth
    that buries and renews. Everywhere the sea

    flings itself against the shore, the great sea
  that widens intolerably. No song
can reach you there, though your version of Earth
   —too far even to say *unbeing, black hole*—
    I trust keeps and comforts: lush oblivion.
     Bright faces pass us in the world we chose.

                —for a daughter, not born

CAESAR'S

The mirrored chair a throne he'd pump
to raise or lower for the height, its lever
the brake on a movie Model T. My mother
propped me in its strict aplomb to see myself

across from myself, myself staring back
while Caesar tucked a sheet reversed
around my neck, so I looked an altar boy,
my surplice unfurled in a pluming bib

while he circled me in his doctor's scrubs.
That first time, the ceiling rose with my wails,
his scissors nosing steel along my ears,
above my eyes, *snip, snip*, and I watched

those clippings rain down like chaff
inside the shop's walls, green, like the walls
in the home where "Pop" lay, his hand
from the prone bed closing cold on mine.

I felt the chair drop, Caesar loosening
the collar from my throat, powder-soft now
with its scent of talcum. Arrayed on the floor
below marble and the seats of waiting men—

my wisps and tufts, soft splinters of me,
with the rest of others fallen and tracked.
And Caesar pacing with his sweeper,
the pen line of his neat moustache, the cut

whispers sifting down his slowly filling bin.

BB

Bright grit, pellet, bead of summeriest bronze
Broken off the string of a furled necklace,
Pearl of my anger's petrifying slough,
I loaded the like of it one by one
One afternoon into the barrel's craw,
Then went for those boys and their mocking names
With my father's tree-target gun, my aim
Honed to the moment when the pupil narrows—

Though no one fell at the glare of my hate,
And my brother trooped me away, the bullet
Of my self's little *i*, rogue period,
Smaller than this box-bound, reddish planet.
I hear thousands falling now, in the first
Drops, the patter, the babble on the roof.

A TRUE STORY

He might be hovering above the Earth,
Cartoon bird held in a paw-like hand.
The stiff arm juts, a flagpole, from its perch.
The whole scene looks a kind of tortured dance,
As when a web flaunts its dandled moth;
Or some sleek cat, its revels ended, hauls
Its trophy up a tree while the raw ground
Circuits the prey's blank eyes, but not for real.
So it was in class every time Mr. Staples

Left the room, and big Lou Angri bolted
From his desk to drag Joe Infantino
To the window, lifting him to the ledge,
All four foot something of him, in one go
And hung his wrenching bones over the edge.
Gentle friends, the room wasn't on the first floor,
And Angri, his name more assured than show,
Swung Infantino while we classmates roared
The approval of the hounds, or Coliseum hordes

Merciless in our thrill it wasn't us
Transported by our weakness into toys.
Though high school is not a Bower of Bliss
Angri was angry, Joe a little boy,
Our homeroom teacher left to take a piss,
And no souls named Pleasure, Wrath, or Sin
Rose when the door opened on this Troy.
Just Staples with a voice like helium:
Mr. Angri, reel Mr. Infantino in.

SWISH

Not yet having perfected his signature
shot, he pantomimes the sweet releases

of his idols—Larry Bird's fadeaway,
Abdul-Jabbar's skyhook, Earl the Pearl's

pull-up jumper. Afternoons after school
he churns his dissonant repertoire

on the pick-up court, the moves he makes
an ephebe's ponderous fingers on the

piano his parents will never own,
or tracings he musters for matchbook ads,

Draw the Pirate, the ball's pimpled Braille
the future he feels in his small palm.

Reverse dribble, and he is the Pearl,
his patented 360 driving for the paint,

a full-tilt pirouette that leaves defenders
swatting air; and now, down low, he's intent

backing in, unstoppable, his long body
suddenly vaulting as he pivots, stilt-legged

but fluid, as though priming for liftoff
from some wide, ethereal prairie marsh,

his arm craned aloft that dips, shoulder down,
in the next possession to Bird seizing

the baseline then pitching back, it seems,
behind the basket, the rubber orb arcing

beyond the power forward's flailing arms—
toward what? Not this opulent dream,

but coinage, a sweet riff on the tongue's tip,
parlance sailing cleanly through the netless rim.

ORPHIC

I love the way the Germans say *Rilke,*
As though an engine were inside the name,
The rolled *R* revving like a motorbike,
The silken catch of wheels like fine lamé
Before it abruptly gutters and cuts,
But somehow runs through into the silence
And onto the other side of language
Where emptiness fills with angels and poems—

And keeps on running, like west to east,
Until the sound returns, a held breath
Exhaled, and air stirs with parts of speech
And words palpable as ephemeral Earth—
Piston, gear shaft, handgrip, slipstream, wings,
And the god's revealed in the rush of things.

GRECO

He'd loom in the lime-circled square of home,
His arched body shadowing the plate
That was shaped—it struck me even then—
Like the diamond sewn on Superman's cape,
And we'd watch in awe at each stung drive
He batted into orbit above the field,
Over the fence, the road, the swing, the slide;
Out, once, entirely into the lake
That looked five hundred feet from where he stood
Staring at the point receding in flight
That soared like a warp drive accruing space
Before it splashed down in our disbelief.

What fifteen-year-old could hit a ball that far?
Greco walked among us, an embodied wish
Of the life we imagined beyond our hopes—
Another Babe, Mantle, Aaron, Mays;
Not one of the crowd, but one the crowd
Eyes like a sleek car behind plate glass,
Or the house you'd build in the bright image
From a glossy spread in *Fortune* or *Life*.
In the batter's box Greco tapped his cleats
As if to mime the dream he would become
And then, his ritual, his signature,
He'd bow, almost kneeling, toward the mound,
To reach with his finger and touch the earth
As though he were charging some great machine
Before rising up, the boyhood myth he was—
Our sandlot Antaeus with the sweet swing,
His power summoned from the humming ground.

Not what you'd expect from a lawn man's son,
If genius can be summoned anywhere:
That modest ranch house down a gravel road
Down the road from ours, cookie cutter homes—
Five rooms, screened porch, the walls knotty pine,
The workingman's answer for elegance.
When I'd go to dinner at Greco's house
His father spread himself at the table's head,
All three hundred pounds in his overalls.
Toothless, he stuttered. Would go house to house
Asking for work. Mowing. Trimming. Barely
Getting the words out. Unprimed syllables
Spluttering like his mower's garbled clutch.
Gap-toothed, gregarious, Greco's mother
Circled us with meatballs, sausage bowls,
A charcoal moustache tracing her lip
Nearly thick as the one her son had grown.
After the meal, Mr. Greco reclined,
A sultan gouached with grass in his chair,
And would not let us rise until custom
Prevailed, and we let pass from our bodies
What he deemed a duly appreciative wind,
Lest the food we had eaten take offense
At our not announcing its place in us.

But on their living room's paneled wall
A print's lithe figure brilliant in its frame
Looked out of place but somehow aptly *there*,
Greco's El Greco, bought more for its name
Than its thrum of color, fluency of line,
Its liftoff from the human, bodies primed

Like heat waves from art's tincture and ash.
It hung across from another face of Christ,
Part rock star, part salesman hawking a heart
That flamed from the pleated drapes of his chest.
But here, crucified, the body seemed to float
Like a pale flame honed from the body's loss,
The eyes already fixed on some high beyond.
I learned years later how the man from Crete
Perfected his skill—the Byzantine
Tempera opening windows to God,
His almond-eyed saints rapt before the Word;
Then sailed to Venice, Rome, the Renaissance
Burning in him, only to find in Spain
The mannerist refined into *mysterium*—
Clouds above Toledo, their heaving folds
Fuming above the city and its gorge,
As if stone itself had drifted into smoke.
And this transfigured man in flight from Earth,
Through flesh the spirit loosening from flesh.
And Heaven stooping at the brush's stroke.

Greco's father died of a heart attack,
His mother sometime after they moved
From the lake with its summer sandlot teams
Of would-be greats, our Greco, the chosen,
Who soon won notice in the wider world,
Scholarships to college and his life's wish,
An offer drafted from the major leagues—
Cut when his knee buckled blocking home,
The collision nailing him to the ground.
No comeback. No college. No Hall of Fame,

But a manager's job at a Penney's store:
Sale Days, Gift Wrap, Men's Wear, Night Shift;
Some weekends at home with the family,
His lightning body thickening at the waist.
Some seemed happy the myth had crashed,
Others looked as if to say what's left to say.
Those are the breaks, an apt reflection
For the weightless burden and the bloodless lash
That most lives come down to before they pass
Into the blind stillness of a sleeper's face—
Oh grace inscrutable, Oh monstrous grace.

A GREEK CUP AT THE MET

In memory of Mark R. V. Southern

This crowd in smoky blackness below the rim
riotous along the tondo's reeling frieze,
which looks spotlit, as if with slip and brush
the painter fashioned revels from utter night,

could be The Yardarm's Dionysian crush
we'd join in Fridays after class—a *jorum*
or two, as the Irish say. And in Hittite,
Latin, Frisian, Hebrew, Norse, Portuguese,

Sanskrit, Saxon, Greek? You could order a pint
in any lingo, as though you'd cracked the genome
that decoded *bodhi* from *Babel*, the Bêche-
de-Mer in glott's scored ogham. *We all speak Greek,*

you'd say, and showed us, tracing from English,
Yiddish, gibberish, through word-hoards in half-light,
threading back as from the plumb line of a name
to the source—your labyrinth of Ithakas

where in each the words we are make their home.
To be on parole with you, *laissez*, lazy,
once again in your *parole*—I'd make that wish
like some errant gob rubbing a phoneme bright

as a lamp: *kalyx*, its breath the aspirate shape
of this crater, its flower, its cave, the form
a root routed, ineradicable, hiding
and bound, the *gist* in the morphologist's dream.

In its wake I'd follow the vessel's curve
past parted parties and the Fates' unfolding glaze
to pull you from the whirlpool where the tide
runs darkest at the narrows and the sea churns;

pull you from the *calyx*, *Khar*, the gaping mouth;
from the *Rhibdis*, swallower, your death its design
and *Dasein*—how you'd love to find in the craw
of the beast a German cognate for *to be*.

Would what gulped you down spew you on high,
and if not here, then on some other lea
where you could be the bard, us your lost crew,
where you've mastered the Esperanto of the gods.

On this meander, Mark, I see you in the brede
incised on ovened clay to the cup's empty brim,
and you're the soul the dolphin's back abides
riding wine-dark tongues of waves into the hush.

QUARTET

After Rilke, Trakl, Hölderlin, and Sachs

1.   *Evening*

Leisurely, the evening sky puts on the robe
held up for it by a crown of ancient trees;
you watch, and the realms move apart like lovers—
one travels heavenward, and the other one falls

and lets you be, not bound to either universe,
nor quite so dark as the house with its silence,
nor wholly so certain as eternity implored,
like whatever it is that becomes a star and rises—

and lets you be (to unravel beyond language)
your life, with its fear and infinity burgeoning,
so that, now walled in, now encompassing all,
it pulsates in you—stone, star, wave, particle.

2.   *All Souls*

Gentlemen, ladies—a scrum of grieving friends—
sow their flowers now, the blue and the red,
on graves where the dusk sun lowers its curtain.
Poor, helpless puppets, they rehearse before death.

How rife with fear they look, how beaten to dust
standing here, shadows behind darkened shrubs.
Cries of the unborn keen in the autumn gusts
and someone watches lights in crazy reelings flitter.

The moans of lovers are breathing in the branches,
and with them rot bodies of a mother and child.
How unreal the roundabout of the living's dance ·
and how strangely mingled with the evening wind.

Their lives are so plagued, brokenhearted, lacerated.
Have mercy, God, on women's torments and despair,
and on these requiems, so hopeless and desolate.
Hushed, the lonely wander through vaulting halls of stars.

3.   *The Way*

Greatness—you wanted it, too, but love hurls
everything down, grief grovels us till we're tame,
though not for nothing are all of us bowed
back to the fetal cringe from which we came.

Go any which way. Somewhere in sacred night
dumb nature sows our pensive brede of days;
just so, bent from hell's own cowering heights—
is there nothing straight, nothing not astray?

I've suffered enough to know this—to my knowledge
never have the heavenly, the upholders of all,
never have they guided me like mortal masters
with care and caution along a level path.

Human, assay everything, so bespeak the Heavens,
so that fed on the living core, you will learn
to give thanks to all that is, and grasp the freedom
to go where you will, having torn your self asunder.

4.   *The Seeker*

Like beings that exist in distant nebulae
we pass, revenants, from dream to dream,
we descend right through the blinding walls
of light bending through its sevenfold prism—

but invisible as glass, at last, and wordless,
the quantum singularity of death
held up in eternity's crystal chalice,
and night's wing beats laid bare, with every mystery.

AS A PHRASE SEWN INTO A HAIR SHIRT

By language
to ascend
what is beyond
all language.

With silence
to remark
what in dark
disturbs silence.

Each sun renews
the horizon's
blank summa.

With one screech
the jay infers
its last word.

THE NET

*Translated loosely from a lost Akkadian tablet
discovered among the ruins of Kush.*

God of the first waters, Ea, listen,
    You who parsed chaos with a net from the day:
        Unfasten your knots, let the swells replenish
From subtlest channels, from the seams of flesh.
    The galaxies circuit in their bright delay.
        The least wind tempts me with what might have been.

———————

This petition you've given is nothing new
    Since nothing is older than the wish to die.
        The dew is famished for the sun's caress
But disappearance does not bring release.
    You long to slip the image from the eye
        But the sky's wide mesh will not acquit you.

LATE BLOOMER

Something whispered I wanted more of myself.
That's how I turned into the *fleur* of myself.

The lake. The ripple's shimmer. That lilting face.
I'll guzzle the infinite pour of myself.

What is this flow I feel, its course through soft bone?
The current? The mother lode? The ore of myself?

Fill me with all things. Empty me completely.
I winnow and still am the store of myself.

Imagine Earth, the stars—all space expanding—
And finding everywhere the core of myself.

If soul's estate means a mansion's many rooms
Then someday I will take a tour of myself.

Do you think me insane, my hypocrite twin?
A catatonic's stare? The whore of myself?

Call me this. Call me that. Call me what you will.
I surpass beyond words the lore of myself.

Time blooms with space, and their sum's all I am.
I am forever the before of myself.

Beauty is Truth, Truth Beauty, Beauty is Truth . . .
X to nth power is the shore of myself.

Narcissus—the name a wind passing through wind.
Now watch me step through the door of myself.

VESPERS MEDITATION AT WELLFLEET BAY

Moored on the glittering fabric of the waves
the boats endure each omnipresent fold
that caves on itself to become the waves
I'm watching now, improvisational waves,
meticulous ripples endlessly unwound,
it seems, from the spool of themselves. These waves
awash in their opulent world of waves
luff the hulls and bound sails stayed by knots
against the wind, though it's mild, and not
one of the gales that sometimes hurls the waves
onto the wharf that I will call my home
for now, as though I had no other home.

The wind and light that make this seascape home
magnetize distance. They also move in waves,
they also travel from some farther home
(if one can call the roiling infinite home),
not outer-ward but deeper in the folds,
the inner amplitudes of bodies—home
apportioned into Timbuktus of home.
Gazing at the bay, one could feel enwound
with such similitudes, but for the wound,
an emptiness in the idea of home.
It's the thinking of it makes the knot
inside the mind, the gut, the mind the knot

unraveling—*You are what this is not,*
though this is all you'll know to be your home.
If swimming through space I saw the blue knot
of the planet floating in what it's not

49

I might feel like I'd been furled in waves,
myself unfurling from the fixed knot
of what I know myself to be, this knot
of particular matter. In the folds
of myself—emergent, aqueous folds—
I tack toward the offing of what I'm not
where everything that is unwinds to be wound
into new signatures that, too, will be unwound.

Knowing this seals the gravity of the wound
one feels—a black hole's all-imploding knot
would be the outward figure of this wound
if somehow the scales could be wound and wound
into a gold intricacy of home
that, by naming it, could cicatrize the wound.
Scale down. Follow to where the strings are wound,
no, wind what is, was, what will be in waves,
the melisma in which the worlds are wound.
Let light's leitmotiv in-wind you in its folds.
There is only this extravagance as it unfolds.

Along the shore the sand grains wash in folds.
Micron by micron they rose, will be wound
down by forces that keep all in their fold.
I feel like Thel on the brink beyond her fold—
How is it all things are what they are not?
And clod and spirit run back to the fold
of Blake's imagined world. The beach unfolds
in broken symmetries—an expanse of home—
shattered shells, shattered stones. Away from home

families tour the wharf; invisible folds
from Wood End ruffle the air in waves.
A young girl kneels along the lulling waves.

Why do we come at dusk to worship waves
when night makes plain its penchant to enfold?
I'd know the name in which all things are wound.
I wish I knew this vastness I am not,
its everlasting flow. Light is always home.

SEEDLINGS FLARING IN FALLOW BEDS

We towered above them, two mortal gods,
   the flags of each little need burgeoning.
The outsized leaves, the pods, the silk greenwood
   looked playground forests where one by one,
imperceptibly, they'd grow by slow motion
   into stalks urgent with light's primal goad;
would, if we allowed them, presume the long
   ascent to mastery of sky and yard.
Kneeling, we pinched each neophyte stem
   until the root came free, without a cry
of course, unlike childhood trees in storm;
   gathered them, jade-leafed, into a torn pile—
innocent as the old saws faith, hope, love.
   This morning, waking, we could barely move

for all our mourning. Awake, the fan moved,
   steady engine, above—Dante said *love*
propelled the sun and other stars. Our pile
   of laundry lay where we left it, a storm
of tangled clothes, sheets, and no child's cry
   calling us to the day. At birth, the stem-
cells begin their slouch to the boneyard,
   body's embodied metaphors, their long
translation the primal protean goad
   into a reaching, clasping hand: the motion
beginning in one, ending in no one.
   Midlife we find ourselves in our dark wood,
abstracted from such rounds of burgeoning—
   out of time, in time, a pair of twilit gods

banished from a time when gods dreamed gods
   and lower worlds rose with the burgeoning:
We would be floor life flourishing in greenwood
   on a shaft of sun. Don't you recall the one
the morning when we sat, leaves in motion
   over our heads. They sounded more the goad
of water rushing from a hidden source, long
   effluent. How it held us there, a halyard
connecting earth to sky, the murmuring stems
   of a real spring engendering the mimicry.
Moss clouds at the hollow. Rootlets in storm.
   And that salamander blended to a pile
of purl-burnished stones. You saw it first, love.
   We watched and watched until we watched it move.

AN ECHO ON THE NARROWS

What are you, Never-to-Be, but my own voice   *Voice,*
returning like light waves from outer space   *space*
while the red-shifting stars accelerate   *accelerate*
beyond eye-shot in the all-freezing distance?   *distance.*

Sometimes I think I see you through dark glass,   *Glass*
plucked into being. And the dream consoles   *consoles*
of infinite strings, of far fields only   *only*
separated like lives beheld at a glance.   *at a glance.*

I want the world to whirl at my embrace;   *Brace*
or better, you are beside a shore yourself,   *yourself.*
your small hands reaching—though the winds are stiff—   *Stiff*
prizing shells between the foam and currents.   *currents*

And I angle my lens for light to hold   *hold*
you in its sight until I am no one.   *no one.*

—for a son not born

FREQUENCY

Intently as caravans along the sunburnt plains
of our television, the elephants

shamble to their burial grounds, the ancient
call of their kind a sound wave they listen

for elusively with their feet, whose leather pads
scan the earth beneath them, iPods

bringing the news; which is more how the muse
came before the hum of cathode tubes,

the whir of satellites—a summoning
felt inside the body and the bones;

or that small voice in the static of belief,
its underscore missed inevitably,

an infinite, brilliantly garbled symphony
all the dials falter from. . . . You lean

against my shoulder while the screen fills
with some new mirage. Rhythmically,

your breathing adjusts its universe
that quietly starts shifting out of phase

beyond the world's surrender and surmise
though intimate as a synapse

flickering on in its own accustomed room,
waiting, love, for word to filter through.

A WORD FROM THE DUVET OUT OF SEASON

Even folded over
inside the trunk with its drift of moths,

still I know myself to be

a hidden lift of wings and cloud life,
the wind's white breath across the snowfield.

WITTGENSTEIN TRIPTYCH

A doubt that doubted everything would not be a doubt.
Ludwig Wittgenstein

Well, God has arrived. I met him on the 5:15 train.
John Maynard Keynes

1.   *The Impossible Box*

The world is everything that is the case
Here on the page with its frozen oceans
Evolving underneath—ice, erotica,
Whole odysseys with their heaving logic
Opened. Such zones are your inheritance.
Return, and watch them kindle into ash.
Leave, and they will stifle to a mezzotint
Drained of all brilliance but nostalgia's
Insurgent stream. Ahead, tumuli
Stud horizons crepuscular with rushlight.
Even so, why not let them linger like a
Vivid inkling in the mind, a birth
Evanescing into this day or that.
Retrace the pattern back to a morning
Yawed from the straight way, zero summer sun
Telescopic, the wind your alibi.
Here is the bright center, your only Earth
Insistent in its passing, luxuriant.
Nothing fills the blue amplitude of sky
Gathering on the offing like a door.
That is where you want to be, a brochure
Homing you far from home, a leitmotiv

Assumed with the figures inside a cave
That flare on a firmament of bosses
Improvised in stone, granite cumuli.
Something in the emptiness of the world
Transmits its secret in the farthest fall—
Hollow sum seething in the quantum blur,
Elapsing summa, the slow dynamo
Composed even unto the bottommost flaw.
Alice fell through her image in glass. One,
Someone, sees past the mirror into hush.
Everything is the case. The world is that.

2.   *A Cottage at Rosro*

In the gospels one finds huts, in St. Paul churches,
And here where Killary opens to the sea
A disused coastguard cottage where the IRA
Hid their prisoners. So you sit shock haired, granite eyed
At the kitchen window, chipping at propositions,
The frames and games of language like a blown gestalt—
The difficulty is to realize the groundless-
Ness of our believing—while, as on every morning,
The caretaker arrives timely with milk and peat
And strews across the floor tea leaves to draw the dirt,
Then gathers the scattered drafts to burn, as if to prove
The lonely genius's trope for how you lived your life:
Philosophy is nothing but tidying up a room.
Though weren't you, too, the private at the searchlight
On the Vistula, waiting for your turn at the front,
The kite maker who as a child schooled with Hitler?
And at the observation post, nightly flak and gunfire,
Nightly expecting to die—*From time to time*
I become an animal—carrying your *Tractatus*
In trenches, prison camps, to the unregarding world?
Giving up your family wealth, you taught the poor;
Taught, when fame came to you, your dons-in-waiting
To turn away from academic life and work
Like a gardener whose spade uproots the wish to die,
For truth cannot be said, it can only be shown.
Which is why now you stand completely absorbed
By the shape you've traced in earth beside the path
Where you walk in the hills above the harbor,

A shape of two aspects in one, like flesh and spirit,
Before you move ahead, thinking of the boat ride
You took the day before, the seabirds, the islands,
How the clouds lifted a moment from one distant ben
And sunlight rioted in silence along the rock face.

3.   *The Resurrection of the Body*

You wanted it for the milkweed you crushed
In your hand, your eyes puzzling from seed
To flower, from flower to seed—*Impossible.*

You wanted it for the need, like an arm lost
In war that the soldier, a pianist, endures
Until in time he keys absence into mastery.

Didn't you say that in order to grow on,
The tree must bend at a knot in the trunk
As though the tree itself were shadow of the sky,

And the spirit driven from the human
By science, by the machine, makes its return
In a mere dawn on the other side of language?

It's a picture that holds us captive, you'd say,
And like some zealous detective in pursuit
You'd grill the propositions, the clues in spate—

A clock is a bewildering instrument
Measuring a fragment of infinity,
Measuring something that does not exist—

While all your life you held at bay the end
Of your passion, this stray student, that friend,
The lovers through whom you kept love crucified.

You wanted it for them, and for the suicides,
Your brothers and the countries left behind,
Ghosting you through a valley of dry bones

In which you rummaged, looking for God—
Thought's virtuoso whistling Schubert, Haydn—
Consumed in a game you could not consummate:

If there is only speculation, then we are in
A hell where we can do nothing but dream,
Roofed in as it were, cut off from heaven.

Though you'd have made mind as penetrating
As the doubter's finger tendered in the Savior
That could touch, touched, the manifest in the trace—

The world is *everything* that is the case.

WRIT IN WATER

Language is a net
In which the world is caught
Skittery in its scales.

In the Book of Nought
All lines are marked *stet*.
Is prevails.

RED SHIFT

Belfast

In the hearth's grate the glow
of newly rendered ash.

Lumpen, oven-burned
as forgotten scones,

the remnant coals
mull and maunder,

molted suns, their cores
plundered, unstokeable.

Though some keep
sundering on,

insistent presence,
like the afterimage

of stars caught
in the fraction life of scans.

Or like my friend's child,
dead, her face

imprinted, too,
by shuttered light

in a score of photos
arranged on the mantle.

Her eyes hold the room
in the scope of each

cut/caught moment—
her gaze, homing,

that warms and wounds
at once. Rapt azure.

Other Earths far off.

IN WAX AND FIRE

For Schrödinger's cat,
and for Jeoffry, Ollie, and Zero, poets' cats

The dead cat bristles inside its box.
The live cat curls inside the dead cat's bones.
Galaxies roll through unimagined zones.
Uncertain eyes scan light's divergent tracks.

Inside the box a hammer stuns the flux
And poison flares along the dying tone.
The dead cat bristles inside its box.
The live cat curls inside the dead cat's bones

For what might be seconds, might be eons,
While atoms ricochet through space like jacks,
And what is is woven through the helix
Of what's not. Is it here or is it gone,

The dead cat bristling inside its box?
A live cat curls inside the dead cat's bones.

A LIGHTBULB

Less than a gnat's hum in the vast expanse,
its inner antennae flame with your need.
At your every return it returns your wants,
this blind, enfrosted eye that lets you see.

Its inner antennae flame with your need
and lightning's white sum. Behind the shade
this blind, enfrosted eye that lets you see
calms with the comforts of a brilliant cave

you return to each night behind your shade
where you mull and move in a bright shower
calm as the comforts of a brilliant cave,
or waves in the wake of a moiling river

that glints along its shoreline like a knife.
At your every return it returns your wants,
those ambient rhythms of gain and grief
less than a gnat's hum. In the vast expanse

what glints along its shoreline like a knife
when the light clicks on feels palpably here
in ambient rhythms of gain and grief,
though it's the finer current you would revere

with each flyblown, intergalactic wave
somewhere roving the universal stir
in all the majesty of light arrayed.
Its hymn haunts quietly of something more,

this blind, enfrosted eye that lets you see.
At your every return it returns your wants,
its inner antennae aflame with your need,
less than a gnat's hum in the vast expanse.

THE LATE SHOW

The films reel on and won't wind back again.
That magic button on your VCR
fires blanks for the wrong cosmic station,
could ply dead letters from galactic blurs
whirling darkly beyond the room's reflection.
Here, pixels hum in economies of flight,
lifetimes figured on the screen's blue glare.
These shadows alive in flickers of light

move like musings in a mind's obsession—
This gaffe, that fear, has made you who you are.
The plots nose by on their bounded ocean
of wrongs, regrets, and unresolved desires.
The stalker with his surly air, his passion
for revenge, almost trumps the family's plight.
The crook that dies alone, the ruthless star,
each shadow alive in its flicker of light,

each pair of haunted lovers, illusions
of loss or hope or want, pass by your stare
that in this numen would seem carved in stone
if you could watch yourself, night's voyeur
attending your own window's incarnation
of a square immersing the world in its sight.
It shines, you'd say, *it is awash and lunar,
my shadow alive in its flicker of light:*

The sun surrounds us but our eyes are tar.
That would be true if Plato were right
and the cave had a portal, and the mirror
lived, more than shadow, a flicker of light.

DOUBLE DUTCH

1.   The Shopper

The shimmering starship liftoff of the mall
attracts her almost daily, stolen flight
from her life's sad orbit, its dishabille.

Here, amidst the trackless music of the aisles,
she feels transport. Down each alluring rack
her cards account the possibilities—

furs and hats and cashmeres, espadrilles and slacks,
till there is nothing that she might have been,
and there is no regret but what she lacks.

Back home her closet-rooms barrow and brim
with everything she's parceled through the years,
the walls charged by some matter, dark, alien,

whose space collapses like a star in reverse—
the black hole hunger of her universe.

2.   *The Drinker*

wants Heaven but has eclipsed the name
with gods that only purify his pain

and make brief paradise of what he feels—
each soaring flight on that to which he kneels.

To journey back as in the parable,
he'll have to somehow forgo being full

by drinking ocean draughts of emptiness
and, his want wanting, find his wanting blessed.

ORPHEUS IN SECOND LIFE

Their blood like mounting drums with every word
you sang, and so the spurned women gathered
in their throats the shrieks that drowned
your voice, which made stones and trees swoon—
then struck, then limb from limb lionized you
in the true primal way until your head,
torn from the scattered mash, floated downstream
with the singing lips, the singing lyre.
Better now that your body's been hacked to bits
to find yourself uploaded to assembling bytes,
to be fashioned in the image of an avatar,
cyber alter ego, from primitives, textures
infinitely pliant as the flesh—childbirth
from olive bark, those blood drops
spawning anemones: your songs within songs.
Here, on the wide virtual continent,
in the teeming city of embodied shades,
you can live the life you might have lived
without the god's ever-pending breath
urging itself inside you. Go out among
the matrix of creations, morphing throngs,
faces primed like yours for a new life,
your skin alive in the digital breeze.
You are anything now you wish yourself to be—
coder, gamer, sculptor, convener of analogs
at embassies salient in the metaverse, its flawless
terms, its portals bright and bloodless.
And when griefers come like fickle gods,
their havoc cannot harm, but only bring
the briefest lag to the lure of one's desire.
How many Eurydices await you here,

incomparably iterative in their scripts
so each time together is first and last,
riskless in the mist and mass of her going.
Yes, Orpheus, better to forget the call
of your own voice, the sorrows of the rocks
and beasts, the ashen procession of leaves,
all that mourns you, and the one in shadow
whose longing outsings your own, tempting you back
to the mauled and makeshift body of the world.

THE TURNPIKE

. . . an expansion,
Like gold to airy thinness beat . . .

You away, and me on the Peter Pan
   heading home from my own required remove,
I'm drawn by the window's broad reflection,
   the traffic passing along it like a nerve—

an endless charge of cars inside the pane:
   the voltage of the real; though as they go
sliding down its long, ethereal sheen
   where the solid world softens into flow

they take on the ghostly substance of a dream
   or, rather, what we picture dreams to be
since when we're in them, they are what we seem,
   and cause us joy or pain as vividly

as the lives we think we live between the lines
   that imprint us and we pass between.
Here, the world inverts. Shades materialize
   and cars speeding left expand a breach

that transports into doubles on the right,
   and those in transit opposite condense
their mirror selves in a second teeming flight
   as if our lightship bus could break such bonds

and matter shatter. Like all things physical
  it's a conjure of parts and energies,
a neverland of haunts inside the skull,
  though saying so won't prevent this child's cries

from jolting with their needful disturbance,
  or the aging woman across the aisle
from leaning in her slackened, palpable face—
  comically, mildly—till the infant calms.

If, as scientists say, we are like hurled stones
  as bounded and bound, dear, by material,
and if our minds resolve into a mist
  we thinly feel to be the actual,

then who's to say the rock is not the air
  it hurtles through, observed from deeper in,
not above. So you and I circuit there,
  firing the inexhaustible engine.

A WAFFLE HOUSE NEAR THE BILTMORE HOUSE

After touring a rich man's flowering lawns
With the summer crowds of other paying guests
Drawn to ogle over what they'll never own—
Olmsted's floral esplanades, a summerhouse
The size of Versailles the railroad baron's son
Built to oversee these bluish, smoky forests
Stretching ridge to ridge in rolling endless waves
(The mogul's inherited glory if not the maid's)—

We drive where we know hash browns are king
And the waitresses shout in diamond demotic
Pull two, scattered, smothered, drop one in the ring.
A grease slick that looks almost amniotic
Glistens along the grill. Plate clatter. A sling
Of scrambled eggs bubbles across, pure Pollock,
Before the flipper fashions them into form
With toast and bacon. For most here, this is home,

Patty melt, chicken steak, All Day Breakfast, grits—
This franchise between the motel and the mall;
Or it's part of a demesne where one feels one fits,
A place one can afford, no plinths and finials.
Up the hill, gilt windows open on terraces,
Gargoyles, and Aurora lights the Entrance Hall.
Dutch marquetry and silk in the Tower Salon,
Bitter's *Boy Stealing Geese* in the Winter Garden . . .

Everywhere, the eye turns to porcelain, Wedgewood,
An emperor's commissioned print, family portraits
In the bedrooms, Music Room, Gun Room—this refuge

From the world a world with its observatory,
Organ loft, armoires, bureaus, rococo rage,
Napoleon's chess set, galleries, tapestries . . .
Who cleaned the forty-three bathrooms; polished
The claw-footed tubs until the toenails shone?

The waitress clears our napkin yolk bouquets,
Smiles and calls us sweetie, and could just be,
Like the corporate owner who runs this chain,
The daughter's daughter's daughter of a laundress
From the chalet sprawled above. We drive away
Down roads whose signage flashes by and passes—
Nothing to the hawk flying high above our car
And heading for the hills, which also do not care.

THE BIRD CLOCK

From its cold perch at twelve, the owl
sings the soul's moot longing.

~

All my life, though I stop my ears—
the laughter of a mockingbird.

~

Deep in the hollow the chickadee's lost,
deep in the hollow of the yard.

~

Church bells at a distance,
though the cardinal's call attends the trees.

~

For the woodpecker: a war in the oak,
a war of one.

~

My old bicycle horn in your throat;
Canada goose, must I ride on forever?

~

First robin, all my life,
to dwell in the child's wish.

~

Sparrow, sparrow—simple song,
you could lose it in the breeze.

~

Too swift for me, kingfisher—your notes
above the street sweeper's grind.

~

Morning, afternoon, chattering,
Aunt Titmouse, only to yourself.

~

Like a waif in a Halloween suit, the oriole
whistling *trick-or-treat*.

~

Birdsong all day, but none burrows deeper
than the great horned owl's.

GUTTER LIFE

Shook, shook, shook—

like the past tense of a breeze
under the eave's scrim,

occasionally a beak's
melodic instrument
lifted up, school bus yellow,
its skittish alto
threading from the impossible
throat,
      then a sudden
tussle of wings

before the errant parent
arrows off
only to return

—how many times?—

while we watched,
just the two of us,
you with your warm intent,
me chattering on
in the skull's
unkempt haven

The body's prime cause
is the soul

—again, again

while the first ticks nick
inside a shell—

the flown song
attending
each nearly weightless
clamorous heart.

ON A RESCUED COPY OF RADNÓTI'S *CLOUDED SKY* AND A SNAPSHOT OF MY PARENTS, 1946

The blood smear across the cover's shattered trim
Where the doomed lovers lean together the way
My parents posed in postwar photographs
Looks like a child's finger-painted swash
Of neon orange, the tantrum I might have made
Across this morning's outing in Sunset Park,
My father in what looks the murdered poet's coat,
My mother beside him, both smiling through the lens
Into the life they'll share, their years together
A winnowing to stack the heart's album of losses.

By then my own anger had grown like a root
The evening she brought it home the year I left,
A gift saved from the incinerator's miscellany
Of patient ash—*You like poetry, you said?*
Is this a book you want? I found it in the trash.
Inside, the poet's terrifying angel whispered
Of saws in the plum trees and how he would end,
Lines flashing hectic on a knife's edge
Quieted by the suddenly limned face of the beloved:
You are permanent within me in this chaos.

What drew her to the bin on her way from work?
Blood's flourish? These two side by side in a scene
From her own past? Though for her husband
There'd be no forced march, no eclogues scrawled
In forest hideouts and prison camps, no mass grave
Where she would dig and find his body and his book—
The book she'd give me in this other life, where love
Failed and failed and failed and still was love.
And behind each couple the bidden leaves
Blur in the gone light and wind and stay unblown.

RAMBLER

I got rambling, got rambling on my mind

The jagged, red confetti
Of glass from my father's head
After he'd crashed the Rambler
Station wagon coming back
Drunk one night from a party,
My brother and I screaming
As the tree fast-forwarded
Into the crazy TV
Of the windshield while he
Dove over us at impact,
Patted like a rain shower
Starting up, drop by drop by
Drop on the grim tabletop
Of the Samaritan's house,
Bloodied gauze, and the sirens
Winding intently toward us
Like a vine of pungent sound,
The kind they call remontant,
Repeat blooms with lax canes
Bramble-like and thornier,
Freely suckering—New Dawn
Or *Rosa wichuraiana,*
That was the dashboard's color,
The same as the bouncy seats
We'd climb over to get to
The way-back where we'd look back
At the highway unreeling

Behind us as our father
Drove us onward to where-
Ever we were going: not
Malibu, not Corsica,
Places they name cars after,
Where he never went, though he'd
Buy those shiny names, wreck them,
Too, like the Fury that was
My mother's face when the cops
Brought us back, shaken, but safe—
I'll kill you, she said, in the
Doorway, *I kill you, you son
Of a bitch,* her voice caving
To the grill of the Rambler,
A chrome mouth that looked hungry
In the driveway, leering out
Of the body's glossy coat,
The body jet-black, bull-wide,
And sprouting wings like something
Out of a myth, out of a
Myth where the hero has to
Find his way back by holding
Onto a thin string, a vine
Of memory that takes him
Out of the monstrous dark, back
To the light to sit beside
A quiet pond, some petals
Floating to the shore, I said
Petals on a sky-blue pond . . .

A GREEN ROAD IN CLARE

The Burren Way

Homesick for more than home, here, astride the sea's genius,
    I long to dissolve in a limestone landscape—
These terraced beds imprinted with grikes, the pillowed clints
    Interleaved with hollows where for eons rainwater's
Patient nibs scribed the chronicles of absence into karst,
    And still do, lines plumbing sidewise underground,
Forming a web of secret caves like halls in a dream house
    I dreamed of in my parents' house long ago.
I cannot go there, but follow the tracks' soft laneway out
    Past stile and waymarking deeper into *boireann*,
The "Place of Rocks," ocean's crushed shells and skeletons formed
    To a horizon risen from the ancient sea.
"Neither tree to hang someone, nor soil enough to bury him,"
    Cromwell lamented, having reached this graven edge,
Though had he looked, he'd have seen graves enough: tombs, raths
    Recalling playthings in a land of make believe,
Now this lost Famine village still deserted and brooding
    Where a surface river tumbles from the shale,
Its roofless walls a thriving quarter of dens and fuchsia.
    My green road itself is like a path through loss
Where Famine roads splintered, directionless, to nowhere,
    For the hungry their work a Relief without relief,
While underneath me it flows on—water's flawless love
    Honing the inner spaces, invisibly, constantly,
So along the outer faults the barren world flourishes—
    Cinquefoil, silverweed, cranesbill, gentian, orchid,
Saxifrage splitting the rocks' dappled stencils of bone.
    Rockroses burst beside the ephemeral lakes.

It's not all death, I think, this double cemetery of earth
　　And thought with its sunken city off the coast,
With its "green hole" by the harbor the locals call Hell,
　　And its cliffs rising from the head of the past
At the spirit's base—"Who is my father in this world?"
　　Or my mother, *Moher, Mothair*, that silent "T"
My central, empty cross? What was it I meant to find
　　Here, now, nowhere, raging in the pitch-pipe wind:
An answer, human, out of the sublime? To be whole again?
　　Song mastering the wake of everything gone?
You are this longing, the iron in the wish for origin.
　　It sounds you, shapes you, water under stone.

CODA: THE LINE

Now fall quickens
To marginless sky,

And these wild geese
Arrowing the Narrows

Could be Zeno's
Imaginary line,

Each moment's point
A fractal integer

Perpetually halved
Until the passage

Brightens the mark
As the mark recedes

Infinitely away,
The way the dead

Make passage
Inside, each life

With their lives
Riding outward

Like Måel Dúin,
Brendan, Bran

Into the limitless
That seems to pause

In the Great Going,
Each hastening span

A well feeding
The annals of loss,

And each life a gloss
From the scribe's nib

Justified
In the needle's eye.

Notes

"Double Exposure" is for Chris Agee.

"And Now Nothing Will Be Restrained from Them": The title comes from the biblical story of the Tower of Babel. Most of the italicized words are from the soon-to-be extinct languages referred to in the poem, except for *frumwoerc* (creation), *fyr* (fire) and *tofts* (homestead), which are from the Anglo-Saxon.

"Greco" is for Mark Jarman and B. H. Fairchild.

"Quartet" combines translated sections of, in sequence, Rilke's "Evening," Trakl's "All Souls," Hölderlin's "Lebenslauf," and Sachs's "The Seeker."

"A Word from the Duvet Out of Season" is for Geraldine Mills and Peter Moore.

"Wittgenstein Triptych": The form of "The Impossible Box" is a four-sided acrostic.

"Writ in Water": Ludwig Wittgenstein is said to have declared, "Language is a net."

"Red Shift" is in memory of Miriam Agee, for Chris, Noirin, and Jacob.

"In Wax and Fire": The Austrian physicist Erwin Schrödinger proposed what is now known as the Schrödinger wave equation to describe the motion of the electron wave, an equation which in turn provided accurate predictions for the behaviors of atoms. At the same time, as a result, it became impossible to separate the observed behavior from the observer. Schrödinger therefore proposed a thought experiment in which a live cat is placed inside a box in which a uranium atom decays, with a fifty-fifty chance of killing the cat. When the box is opened, the wave function collapses and the cat is either dead or alive through the act of observation—for Schrödinger an absurdity.

"Orpheus in Second Life": Second Life is a virtual world accessible on the World Wide Web. In Second Life, one designs an avatar for oneself, or multiple avatars, out of "primitives," templates of script that are elaborated into any form desired. In the lingo of Second Life, "griefers" are participants who cause others trouble. In Ovid's account Orpheus is reunited with his wife, Eurydice, in the Elysian Fields after the maenads kill and dismember him.

"On a Rescued Copy of Radnóti's *Clouded Sky* and a Snapshot of My Parents, 1946": The Hungarian Jewish poet Miklós Radnóti was killed on a forced march by the Nazis in 1944. A notebook containing the poems for his posthumous book *Clouded Sky* was discovered in his coat pocket after his body was exhumed from a mass grave.

"Rambler" is for Afaa Michael Weaver. The epigraph is from his poem "Rambling."

"A Green Road in Clare" and "Coda: The Line" complete the book-length sequence of *The Narrows*. "Coda: The Line" should be read as the first poem in section XI before "The Rainbow Café," and "A Green Road in Clare" should be read as the last poem of the same section, after "Afterlives."

Acknowledgments

Agenda (England), *Agni, Boulevard, Cimarron Review, The Common, Confrontation, Crab Orchard Review, The Cresset, The Evansville Review, Great River Review, The Hudson Review, Ibbetson Street, Image, Iron Horse, Literary Imagination, Natural Bridge, New South, Poetry East, Poetry Ireland, Post Road, Salamander, Salmagundi, The Sewanee Review, Solstice Literary Magazine, The Southern Review, Southwest Review, Sou'wester, Stand* (England), *32 Poems, Valparaiso Review,* and *Virginia Quarterly Review.*

"The Turnpike" appeared in *Best American Poetry 2012.*
"Late Bloomer" appeared in the Alhambra Poetry Calendar 2011.
"Vespers Meditation at Wellfleet Bay" appeared in Alhambra Poetry Calendar 2013.

I want to thank Bruce Beasley, Christine Casson, Martha Rhodes, William Thompson, and William Wenthe for their help with some of the poems in this book, and for suggestions about ordering.

Daniel Tobin is the author of five previous books of poems, *Where the World Is Made, Double Life, The Narrows, Second Things,* and *Belated Heavens* (winner of the Massachusetts Book Award in Poetry, 2011), along with the critical studies *Passage to the Center* and *Awake in America.* He is the editor of *The Book of Irish American Poetry from the Eighteenth Century to the Present, Light in Hand: The Selected Early Poems of Lola Ridge,* and (with Pimone Triplett) *Poet's Work, Poet's Play: Essays on the Practice and the Art.* His awards include the "Discovery" / The Nation Award, the Robert Penn Warren Award, the Robert Frost Fellowship, the Katharine Bakeless Nason Prize, and creative writing fellowships from the National Endowment for the Arts and the John Simon Guggenheim Foundation.